What was it?

turn
to see

A beach ball.

Catch!

What Was It Before It Was Smashed?

by Kristen McCurry

PEBBLE
a capstone imprint

What do you think these things were
before they were smashed?

Take a guess,
then turn each page to find out!

What was it?

turn
to see

What was it?

turn
to see

What was it?

turn
to see

Pennies.

How many can you count?

What was it?

turn
to see

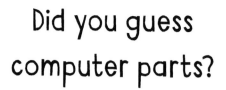

What was it?

turn
to see

Eggs.

Crack!

What was it?

turn
to see

Birthday cake.

Yum!

What was it?

turn
to see

What was it?

turn
to see

Cans.

Cans are crushed before they are recycled.

What was it?

 turn to see

What was it?

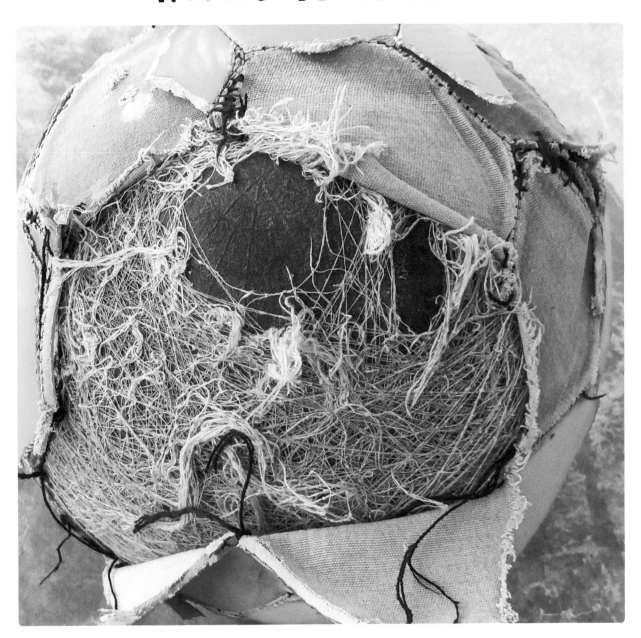

 turn to see

What was it?

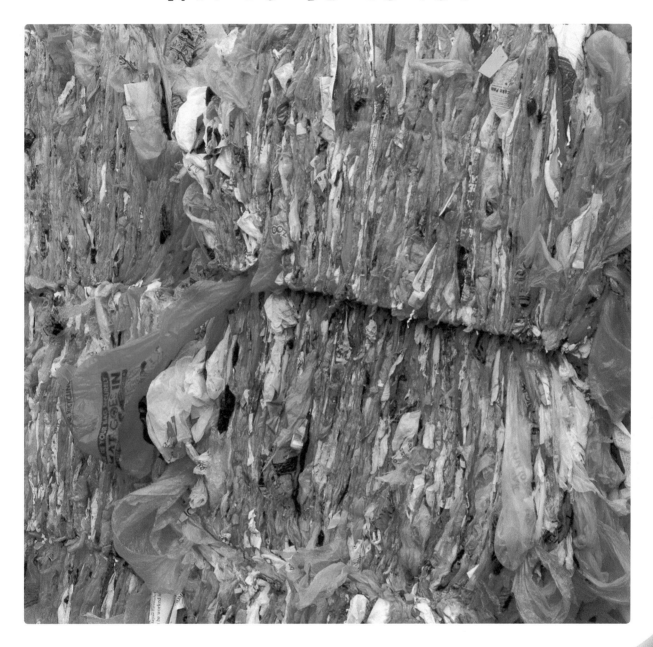

turn
to see

What was it?

 turn to see

What was it?

turn
to see

Good job! Try all the books in this series!

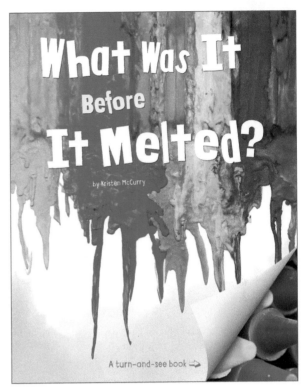

Pebble Sprout is published by Pebble, an imprint of Capstone.
1710 Roe Crest Drive
North Mankato, Minnesota 56003
www.capstonepub.com

Library of Congress Cataloging-in-Publication Data.
Names: McCurry, Kristen, author. Title: What was it before it was smashed? / Kristen McCurry.Description: North Mankato, Minnesota : Pebble Sprout, a Capstone imprint, [2020] | Series: What was it? | Audience: Ages 4-8. | Audience: Grades K-1. | Summary: "Crush, crash, smash! Photo puzzles featuring mashed and mangled objects give pre-readers a mystery to solve...what was it before it got smashed?"-- Provided by publisher. Identifiers: LCCN 2019044101 (print) | LCCN 2019044102 (ebook) | ISBN9781977113337 (hardcover) | ISBN 9781977120151 (paperback) | ISBN 9781977113375 (ebook)Subjects: LCSH: Picture puzzles--Juvenile literature. | Visual perception--Juvenile literature.Classification: LCC GV1507.P47 M379 2020 (print) | LCC GV1507.P47 (ebook) | DDC 793.73--dc23LC record available at https://lccn.loc.gov/2019044101LC ebook record available at https://lccn.loc.gov/2019044102

Designer: Sarah Bennett
Media Researcher: Eric Gohl
Production Specialist: Tori Abraham

Image credits
Capstone Studio: Karon Dubke, 15, 16; Shutterstock: Africa Studio, 8, aga7ta, 13, Anakumka, 21, AsiaTravel, 20, Awe Inspiring Images, 25, Brian A Jackson, 4, fizkes, 30, Fotos593, 28, Frank Filiatreau, 10, Fritzphoto, 7, Grossinger, 26, GUNDAM_Ai, 12, Huguette Roe, 27, Jeab Ploykrachang, 24, JN Rem, 5, Jonathan Pais, 9, Kirby Leigh, 17, Kristyna Vagnerova, 18, MarcoFood, 1, Mike Plotczyk Images, 19, Mindscape Studio, 22, Payu Sriwong, 23, Rigucci, 6, SAJE, 3, Shulevskyy Volodymyr, 14, Tatiana Volgutova, cover, vilax, 11, ymgerman, 29, yuris, cover (bottom right)

Design Elements: Shutterstock